Dragonflies

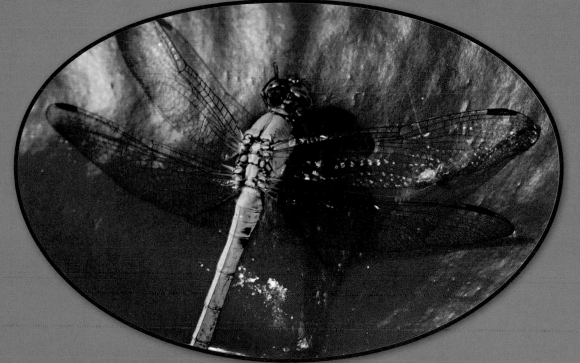

Rebecca Rissman

www.raintreepublishers.co.uk
Visit our website to find out
more information about
Raintree books.

To order:
☎ Phone 0845 6044371
▤ Fax +44 (0) 1865 312263
✉ Email myorders@raintreepublishers.co.uk

Customers from outside the UK please telephone +44 1865 312262

Raintree is an imprint of Capstone Global Library Limited, a
company incorporated in England and Wales having its registered
office at 7 Pilgrim Street, London, EC4V 6LB – Registered company
number: 6695582

Edited by Dan Nunn, Rebecca Rissman, and Catherine Veitch
Designed by Joanna Hinton-Malivoire
Picture research by Mica Brancic
Originated by Capstone Global Library Ltd
Production by Victoria Fitzgerald
Printed in China by South China Printing Company Ltd

ISBN 978 1 406 24135 8 (hardback)
16 15 14 13 12
10 9 8 7 6 5 4 3 2 1

ISBN 978 1 406 24149 5 (paperback)
17 16 15 14 13
10 9 8 7 6 5 4 3 2 1

British Library Cataloguing in Publication Data
Rissman, Rebecca.
Dragonflies. – (Creepy crawlies)
595.7'33-dc22
A full catalogue record for this book is available from the
British Library.

Acknowledgements
We would like to thank the following for permission to reproduce
photographs: Dreamstime p. 22 (© Alexey Romanov); FLPA pp.
18, 19 (Minden Pictures/FN/Rene Krekels); iStockphoto pp. 8b (©
Steve McGuire), 9b (© Tan Kian Khoon), 15a (© Kelvin Yam), 16 (©
Manit321); Shutterstock pp. 1 & 14b (© Jason Patrick Ross), 5 & 23
(© night_cat), 6 (© Rob Hainer), 7 (© Tharkul), 8a (© Joanna22),
9a (© Gnilenkov Aleksey), 10 (© kurt_G), 11 (© Ant's Perspective
Photography), 13 & 22 (© alslutsky), 14a (© Tomas Sereda), 15b
(© ClimberJAK), 17 (© Christian Musat), 21 (© William Attard
McCarthy), 22 (© irin-k, © Vital Che, Henrik Larsson), 23 (© Alex
Staroseltsev, © Photolinc, © photolinc).

Cover photograph of a close-up of a dragonfly reproduced with
permission of Shutterstock (© defpicture).

Every effort has been made to contact copyright holders of any
material reproduced in this book. Any omissions will be rectified in
subsequent printings if notice is given to the publisher.

The publishers would like to thank Michael Bright for his assistance
in the preparation of this book.

Contents

Let's search!

Did you see that blur
rushing through the sky?

What could it be?
Oh, it's a dragonfly!

Dragonflies have big, coloured eyes to help them see around.

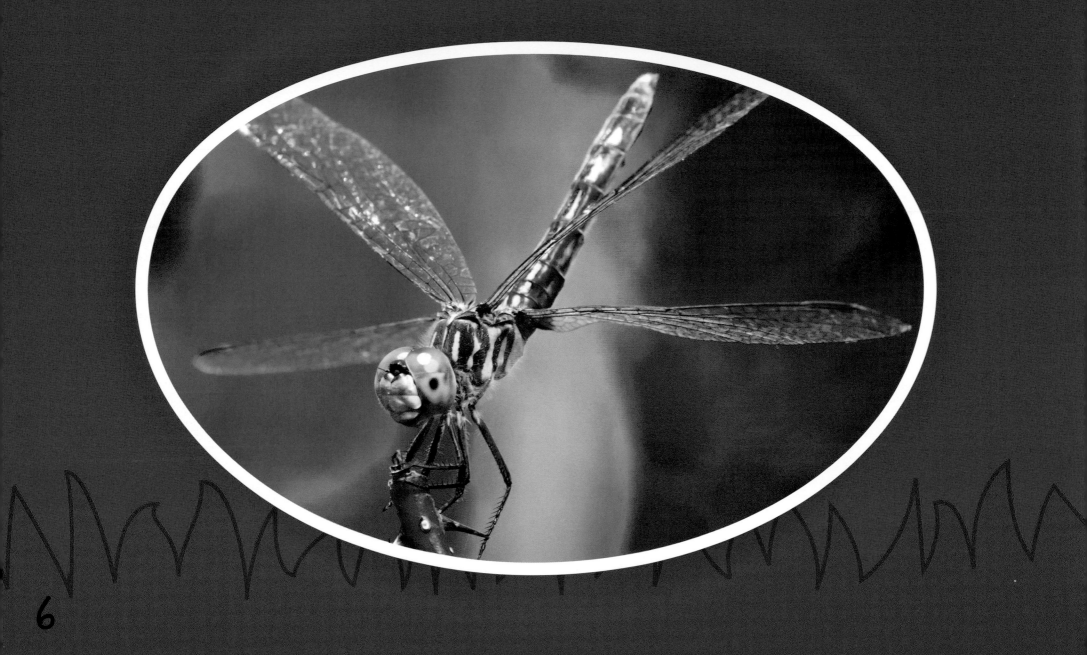

eyes

Their big eyes spot food in the sky and also on the ground.

7

Have you ever seen a dragonfly sitting close by?

They come in so many shapes and sizes! Watch them as they fly.

Dragonflies have two antennae, but they are very small.

Unless you look quite closely, you might not see them at all!

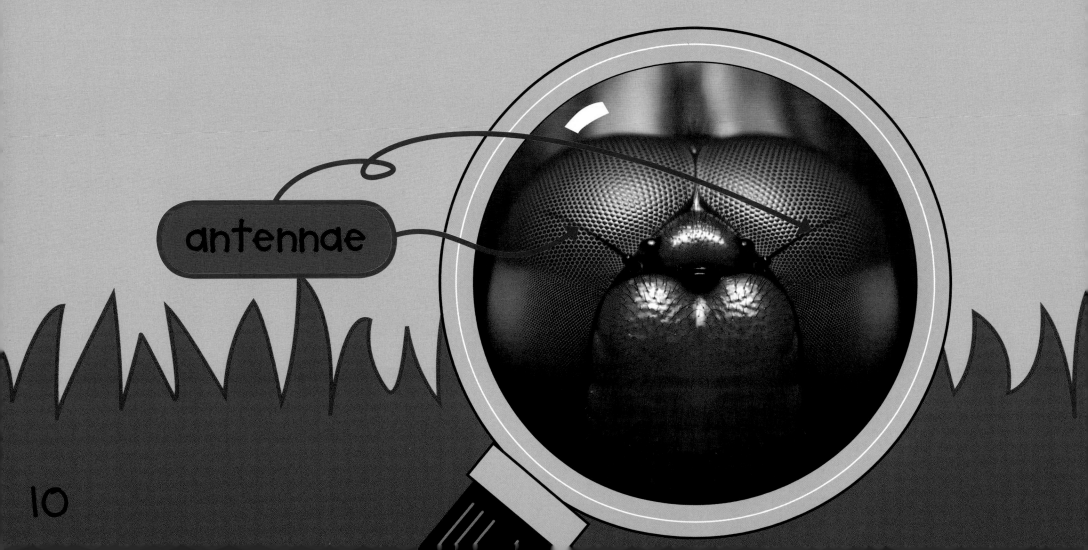

antennae

How many wings do you see on this dragonfly? 1, 2, 3, and 4.

Its four strong wings help the dragonfly to soar!

What colour are dragonflies?
Are they dull or are they bright?

Red, blue, pink, or orange.
Dragonflies make a pretty sight!

Dragonflies don't just fly.
They also walk and climb.

Their six legs help them to
move around in record time!

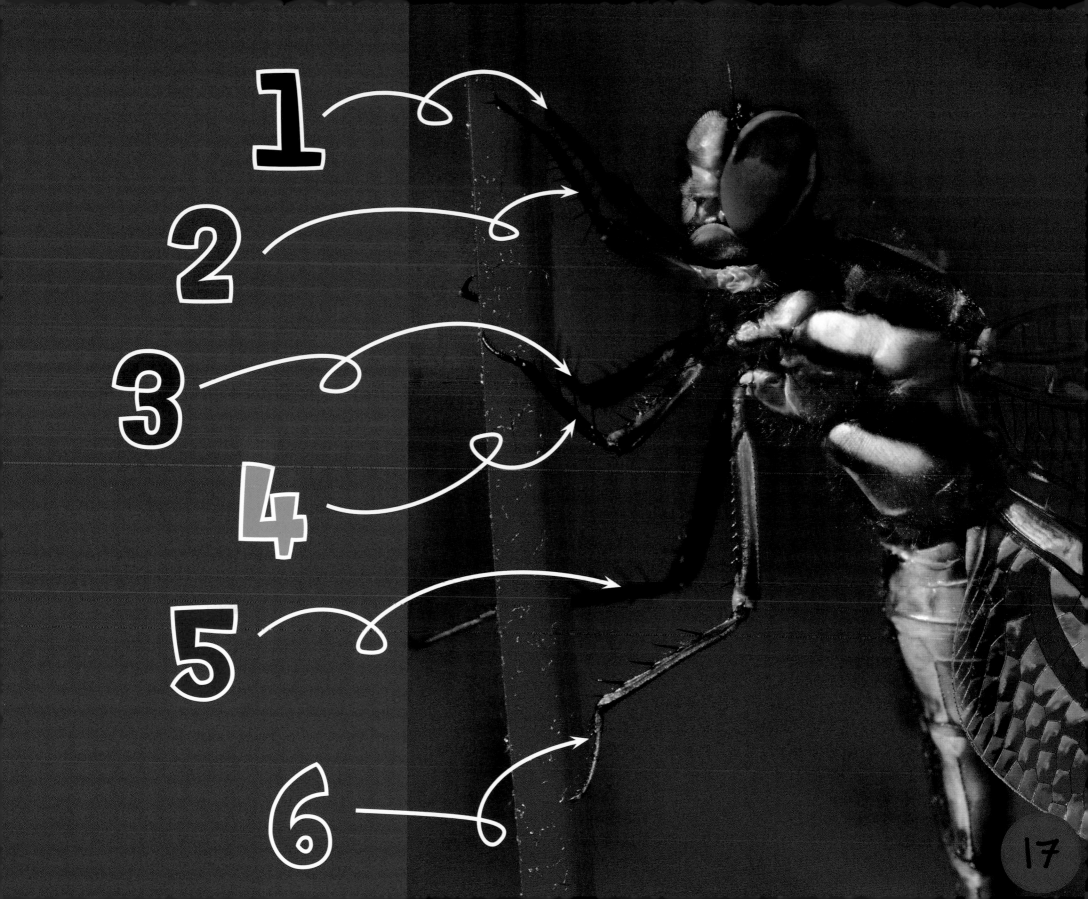

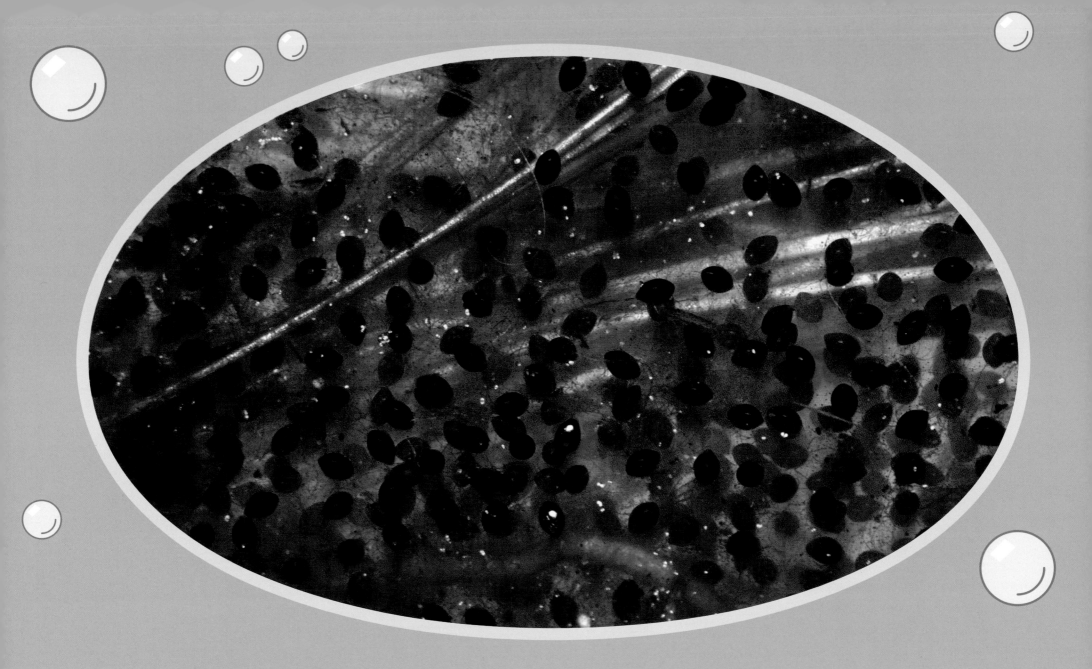

Dragonflies lay eggs in water, which hatch into babies there.

These little nymphs soon become dragonflies that fly through the air!

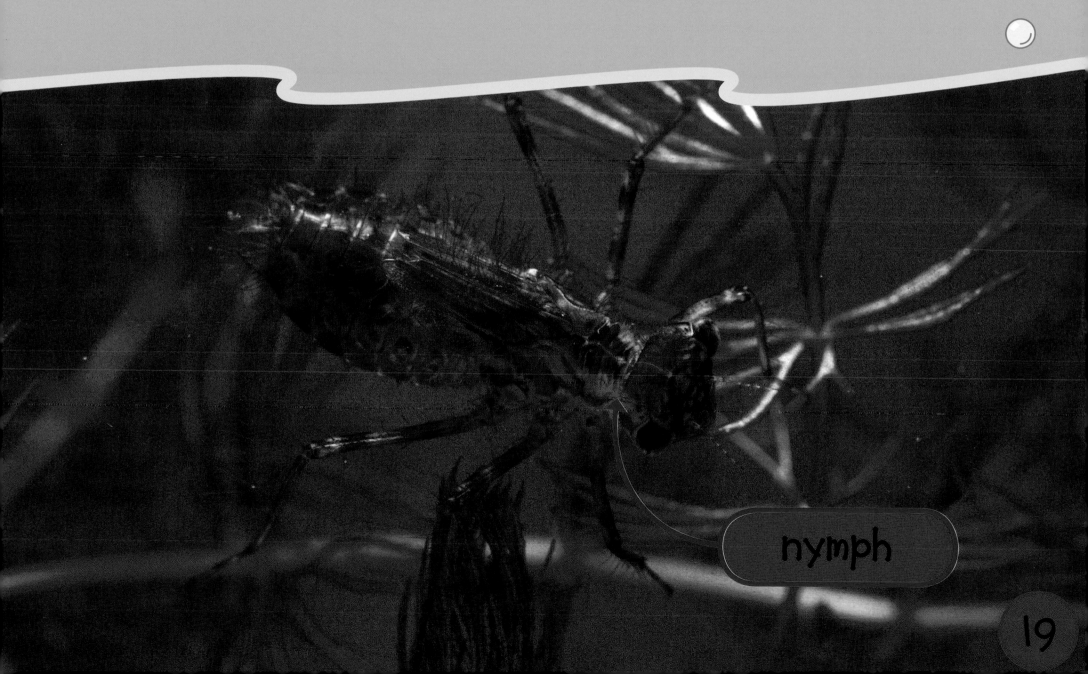

nymph

Dragonflies like all water,
or that's the way it seems!

Look for dragonflies if you're near
big puddles, lakes, or streams!

Counting dragonflies

How many dragonflies can you count?
Some are brown and some are blue.

Look for dragonflies all around,
and you could find quite a few!

Did you know?

Dragonflies can fly backwards.

Index